D0458141

116532854

NATIVE AMERICAN LEADERS OF THE WILD WEST

GERONIMO
✤Apache Warrior✤

William R. Sanford

ENSLOW PUBLISHERS, INC.

Bloy St. & Ramsey Ave.	P.O. Box 38
Box 777	Aldershot
Hillside, N.J. 07205	Hant GU12 6BP
U.S.A.	U.K.

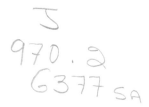

Library of Congress Cataloging-in-Publication Data

Sanford, William R. (William Reynolds), 1927–
    Geronimo, Apache warrior / William R. Sanford.
        p. cm. — (Native American leaders of the Wild West)
    Includes bibliographical references and index.
    ISBN 0-89490-510-4
    1. Geronimo, 1829–1909—Juvenile literature. 2. Apache Indians—
Biography—Juvenile literature. 3. Apache Indians—Kings and
rulers—Juvenile literature. 4. Apache Indians—History—Juvenile
literature. I. Title. II. Series: Sanford, William R. (William
Reynolds), 1927–   . Native American leaders of the Wild West.
E99.A6G3272 1994
979'.004972'0092—dc20
[B]   93-42257
                                                            CIP
                                                             AC

Printed in the United States of America

10 9 8 7 6 5 4 3 2 1

Photo Credits: Fort Sill Museum, pp. 15, 19, 27, 33, 37, 40, 41; National
Archives, pp. 6, 11, 12, 28, 31, 36, 39; William R. Sanford, pp. 10, 16, 20, 23,
25.

Cover Illustration: Paul Daly.

═══CONTENTS═══

AUTHOR'S NOTE

This book tells the true story of the Apache warrior, Geronimo. Many mistakenly think the great warrior led all the Apaches. But his true fame rests on his leadership of only a relative few. After the deaths of the Apache chiefs Cochise and Mangas Coloradas, the press raced to print stories about Geronimo. Some were made up, but others were true. The events described in this book all really happened.

World War II brought a new kind of warfare. Soldiers dropped from planes by parachute onto enemy soil. As they jumped, they recalled the Apache raider who struck without warning. They shouted: Geronimo!

MASSACRE IN MEXICO

Geronimo—the Apache warrior scowls at us from his photos. A barrel chest tops his five-foot, eight-inch frame. His nose is like the beak of a hawk. His eyes resemble black glass. Jutting cheekbones and a slit of a mouth add to his glare. What made him so fierce?

As a child, Geronimo learned of the hatred between Apaches and Mexicans. For centuries the Mexicans had captured his people and made them slaves. The Apaches struck back. They raided Mexican ranches and towns. They herded off horses and cattle. Raiding became a normal way of life. To the Apaches, these raids were lawful and just.

The Mexicans wanted to wipe out the Apaches. They offered money for every Apache scalp. In 1837 the Mexican state of Chihuahua offered 100 pesos (about $100) for each scalp of an Apache warrior. The state would pay

The Apache war leader, Geronimo, brought fear to settlers throughout the Southwest. This fierce warrior is remembered for his raiding and breakouts from reservation life.

fifty pesos for a woman's scalp and twenty-five pesos for a child's. Other states made similar offers.

The United States and Mexico were at war from 1846 to 1848. At the end of the war, the peace treaty made the Southwest part of the United States. About this time, one Mexican state—Chihuahua—tried to end the Apache raids. It urged the Apaches to come and trade for what they wanted.

Geronimo went with his band to the Mexican frontier town of Janos. The Apaches camped in the dry hills outside of town. They planned to trade hides and furs for cloth, knives, and guns. They also hoped to sell the livestock they had stolen in Sonora. Most of the men walked to town to trade. The Apaches did not trust their hosts. They left a small guard to protect the women and children.

The town had gifts for the Apaches. It gave them sacks of supplies. It also gave them bottles of liquor. These the Apaches opened at once. Soon many Apaches were drunk. They staggered back to camp. Geronimo brought gifts for his three children. He gave his supplies to his wife, Alope.

The next day the town again gave gifts. Both sides were happy. The town thought it had bought peace cheaply. The Apaches got supplies without raiding. Geronimo and the others walked toward camp. Women and children ran to them screaming. Mexican soldiers had attacked their camp. They were still there.

Troops from Sonora had crossed the Chihuahua state line. Outside Janos, they came upon the Apache camp. They killed all the guards. They slaughtered more than 100 women and children. Some Apaches scattered into the brush hiding there until dark. When the soldiers left, they took with them 100 captive Apache women and children. In the towns to the south, they would sell them as slaves.

Only eighty warriors remained. They had no arms or supplies with which to fight. They hid in a thicket until the troops had gone. Late that night, they entered the camp. Geronimo said, "I found that my aged mother, my young wife, and my three small children were among the slain. There were no lights in camp. Without being noticed, I silently turned away. I stood by the river. How long I stood there, I do not know."[1]

The Apaches left their dead on the field. The next day, they headed north. Geronimo would never forget what happened at Janos. For the rest of his life, he would seek revenge.

GERONIMO BECOMES
A WARRIOR

The Apaches called themselves the *Diné* and *Indé*, which mean "the people." The name *Apache* comes from the Zuní *Apacheu*. It means "enemy." The Apaches believe that the sun created them. Historians say the Apaches came to the Southwest from western Canada. At their peak in the 1800s, there were about 12,000 Apaches. They divided themselves into six groups. The Apaches built no cities. They moved from place to place. Their land could not support year-round farming.

Geronimo said that he was born in June 1829. He placed his birth in No-doyohn canyon in southeast Arizona. His name at birth was Go Khla Yeh (One Who Yawns). It was the Mexicans who called him Geronimo (Spanish for "Jerome"). No one knows why the Mexicans gave him this name. Geronimo was the grandson of Chief Mahko. His father was Taklishim (The Gray

One) and his mother, Juana. They belonged to a group of Apaches known as the Bedonkohe.

Geronimo lived in a land of searing deserts, blue mountains, and deep canyons. In this harsh land, only the strong and clever survived. He grew up with one sister, Nah-de-ste, and six cousins. The young boys and girls helped gather roots, wild fruit, and nuts. They worked with their parents in the fields. Each family had a small garden plot. Beans and pumpkins grew between rows of corn. In the fall, they carried the harvest to the mountains. There they sealed the food in caves until needed.

At age five or six, Geronimo began training to be a

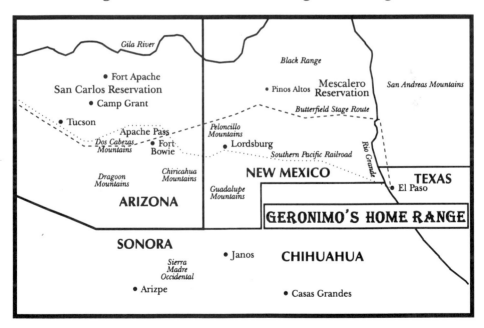

The Apache homeland stretches from Arizona, New Mexico and Texas into northern Mexico.

The Apaches used cradleboards during their babies' first few months of life. The infant was wrapped in swaddling and carried on the back of its mother.

warrior. He made weapons and tools. He took care of the horses. Geronimo learned to hunt small game with a bow and arrows. By the time he was fourteen, he hunted with the men. They taught him the skills of war. He learned to shoot, dodge, hide, and track. On the prairies, he hunted deer, elk, and antelope. Often he hunted cougar. Geronimo killed several of the big cats with a bow and arrows. One he killed with a spear. He used the animal hide to make quivers for arrows. Hunting parties traveled great distances to find buffalo. On horseback, the hunters rode into the herd. At close range, they

Upon marriage, the husband usually joined the family of his wife. The women were responsible for gathering and preparing food, overseeing moves, and producing clothing.

loosed their spears and arrows. They brought back the hides to use as bedding and covers for tipis.

As a child, Geronimo never saw a white person. When in his teens, he joined Chief Juh in raids on ranches and pack trains. The raiders crossed open spaces only at night. During the day, they hid in the mountains.

They took with them a week's supply of dried meat. In camp, Geronimo stood guard duty, fetched wood, and cooked.

After a long illness, Geronimo's father died. Juana did not remarry. Although he was still a young man, Geronimo became the head of the family. He and Juana went south to Mexico. There they would live with his cousin Ishton and her husband, Chief Juh.

Geronimo became a warrior at age seventeen. He said, "Now I could marry the fair Alope, daughter of Noposo. She was a slender, delicate girl. We had been lovers for a long time."[1] Noposo asked Geronimo to pay many ponies for Alope. A few days later, Geronimo appeared at Noposo's lodge. He had the herd of ponies. Alope was now his. The couple returned to Arizona. There they built a buffalo-skin tipi. Alope covered the hides with paintings. In a few years, they had three children. When Geronimo went to Janos to trade, he took his wife and children with him.

GERONIMO TAKES REVENGE

After the massacre at Janos, Geronimo's band fled north. For two days and three nights they did not stop. When they reached the border, they rested. A few days later, Geronimo reached his home. He saw Alope's paintings on the tipi. His children's toys lay scattered inside. Geronimo burned his tipi, and all that was in it.

One day, he left his village alone. He sat with his head bowed, weeping. He heard a voice call his name four times. (Four is the magical Apache number.) The voice said, "No gun can ever kill you. I will take the bullets from the guns of the Mexicans. I will guide your arrows."[1] Geronimo knew he had received a special power. All his life, he had faith in his power. He would receive many wounds. None were fatal.

A year later, in 1859 the Apaches were ready to strike back. Geronimo talked to three bands. Each agreed to go on the warpath. Mangas Coloradas (Red-Sleeves) would lead the Bedonkohe. Others would follow Cochise and Juh. The warriors applied war paint to their faces. War bands held back their hair. They blackened their knives with soot.

The warriors traveled with light loads. Each wore moccasins and a cloth that doubled as a blanket. They carried only their weapons and three days' food. Geronimo guided the warriors through the mountains and valleys. They avoided roads and trails.

Once in Sonora, the war party bypassed many small towns. Outside Arispe, the Apaches killed eight men. They hoped this would draw the soldiers out of the city.

On horseback, Geronimo led his band through the mountain and desert vastness of the Southwest. He was able to cover vast distances, and to find water where none seemed to exist.

The rider is arriving at an Arizona ranch. He warns that the Apaches are about to attack. The artist Frederic Remington traveled to Arizona to cover the campaign against Geronimo.

The Apaches would be waiting. That night, the Apaches captured a supply train. It provided needed guns and supplies.

The next morning, four companies of soldiers came out. Geronimo recognized them as the soldiers who had killed his family. He told this to the chiefs. They allowed him to direct the battle. Geronimo arranged the Apaches in a crescent. They lay hidden in timber. The Mexicans advanced and opened fire. Geronimo sent warriors to attack the Mexicans' rear. At the same time, he led a frontal attack.

The battle was almost over. Geronimo and three others stood in the center of the field. His arrows were all gone. His spears had broken off in the bodies of the dead. Geronimo fought with his knife and bare hands. He recalled:

> *Two armed soldiers came upon us from another part of the field. They shot down two of our men. We, the remaining two, fled toward our own warriors. My companion was struck down by a saber. I reached our warriors, seized a spear, and turned. The one who pursued me missed his aim and fell by my spear. With his saber, I met the trooper who had killed my companion. We grappled and fell. I killed him with my knife and quickly rose over his body. I brandished his saber, seeking for other troopers to kill. There were none.*[2]

In the two-hour battle, the Apaches had killed all the Mexican troops. Geronimo said, "I could not call back my loved ones. I could not bring back the dead Apaches. But I could rejoice in this revenge."[3]

BATTLING MEXICANS
AND MINERS

This victory did not end Geronimo's desire for revenge. He would always hate those who had killed his family. Geronimo soon remarried. Chee-Hash-Kish was a member of Cochise's tribe. Geronimo followed Apache custom. He lived with his wife's band in southeastern Arizona.

Geronimo led small raids into Mexico. Cochise did not mind. To him, these were attacks on ancient foes. Once, Geronimo and two others saw five horses. The animals were tied at the edge of a town. The warriors crept up close to cut the reins. Gunfire poured from nearby houses. Geronimo's friends fell dead. He, however, escaped unhurt. Mexicans pursued him. For two days and nights, he did not eat or drink. At last he threw his pursuers off his track.

A second raid in 1860 also ended in failure. On his

way home from the raid, Geronimo saw a troop of soldiers cross the border. The Mexicans were coming to kill Apaches. He warned his village in time. The Apaches killed eight soldiers. The rest fled south. Geronimo and twenty-five warriors followed their trail. In a mountain pass, the Apaches caught up with them. The soldiers crouched behind their horses. Geronimo led a charge. Hand-to-hand fighting followed. A soldier hit Geronimo in the head with his gun butt. Geronimo fell to the ground. Another Apache killed the trooper with a spear. Geronimo was weak from loss of blood. He barely found the strength to return north.

Geronimo's raids embarrassed the United States.

At times, Geronimo did wear buckskin and a feather headdress. More usually, he wore a head band and clothing made of wool or cotton.

Geronimo and his band return with loot from a raid.

This country had made a promise to Mexico that it would end Apache raiding. But this did not happen. In 1853, the United States signed the Gadsden Purchase. A section of the treaty canceled the promise to stop the raids.

In the late 1850s prospectors found gold in New Mexico. The mines were in the Apache homeland. The miners feared and hated the Apaches. They thought they were "savages." Many felt "The only good Apache is a dead Apache." They wanted to shoot them on sight.

Chief Mangas Coloradas did not want to fight the miners. He tried a trick to get them to leave. Each time he met a miner, he told a story of a rich lode of gold. Each time, the gold was in a different place. All the places lay far away. The miners compared notes. They saw that the chief was lying. They tied the chief to a tree. Then they lashed him with bullwhips. Mangas Coloradas escaped. He then joined Cochise and Geronimo on the warpath. The Apaches captured the miners' supplies. In an attack on a wagon train, they killed sixteen drivers. They also took hundreds of sheep and cattle.

Warfare between the U.S. Army and the Apaches began in early 1861. Cochise and five other warriors visited the soldiers' camp in Apache Pass. An officer arrested Cochise. He accused him of kidnapping an American boy. The chief whipped out his knife. He slashed the tent wall and escaped. He had to leave the other warriors behind.

Geronimo helped Cochise attack a freight train. Soon gunfire filled Apache Pass. The warriors took three Americans captives. Cochise offered to swap them for the captive Apaches. But the plan failed. Both sides killed their prisoners. Then the Apaches faded into the mountains.

In April 1861, the Civil War began. The U.S. Army pulled its troops out of the Southwest in July 1861. It needed them elsewhere. The Apaches knew nothing of the Civil War. They saw the soldiers leaving. They thought they had won their first fight with the Army.

THE APACHES
UNDER ATTACK

For a few months, the Apaches raided at will. Geronimo was among those who attacked Pinos Altos, New Mexico. The miners and settlers fled. No whites remained in this part of the Apache lands.

In the summer of 1861, Southern troops marched into the state. Their leader, Colonel John Taylor, hated all Native Americans. He issued an order. It read: "You will . . . persuade the Apaches to come in for the purpose of making peace. When you get them together, kill all the grown Indians. Take the children prisoners. Sell them to defray the expense of killing the Indians."[1]

Early in 1862, Union troops from Colorado drove the Southern force back to Texas. Then 1,800 Union soldiers arrived from California. On July 14 of that year, 126 Union troops entered Apache Pass. The soldiers needed water from the spring there. On the rocky slopes,

Cochise lay in wait. With him were 700 warriors. It was the biggest force the Apaches ever mustered. Many warriors had rifles. They built stone breastworks with firing slits. The Apaches let the soldiers near the spring. Then they opened fire. The first volley dropped many Army horses. The soldiers wheeled two cannons into place. Twelve-pound shells exploded over the Apaches' heads. Shrapnel ripped into them. Cochise ordered a retreat. The next day, the soldiers continued on their way. It is not clear whether Geronimo fought in the battle. Some say he was raiding in Mexico.

In 1888, Harper's Weekly published this sketch by Remington. It shows the uniform of a typical frontier cavalry officer during the campaign against Geronimo.

General William Carleton tried to end the Apache war. At first he tried to kill all Apaches. Later, he said they could go on a reservation. In the winter of 1862-63, he subdued the Mescaleros. They would go to Fort Sumner to live. Others went to Pinos Altos to give up themselves. Their leader, Mangas Coloradas, entered the town. The miners took him captive. They took him to nearby Fort McLane. That night, soldiers heated bayonets in the fire. They put the bayonets to Mangas Coloradas' feet and legs. When he yelled out, they shot and killed him. Then one of the soldiers scalped him.

Geronimo's influence grew. He was not a chief. Still, chiefs sought his advice. His band stayed away from the whites. They heard strange stories. The Apaches should agree to give up. Then the whites would give them land. There was a catch. They would have to agree to stay on that land. That offer did not tempt them. The band had enough supplies. They led their lives simply.

This changed in one day. Some soldiers found Geronimo's band. They launched a surprise attack. Four warriors fell dead. The soldiers killed five women and seven children. The Apaches lost their supplies, blankets, horses, and clothing.

Soldiers and armed civilians tracked Geronimo's band. They kept them on the move. The army attacked them time after time. Winter was coming. Geronimo said it was the coldest he ever knew.[2] He led his band to safety in New Mexico. Victorio, new chief of the Warm Springs Apaches, welcomed them.

For the next two years, Geronimo raided in Mexico. At Casas Grandes, the town leaders offered to make peace. They gave the Apaches liquor. When they were drunk, two companies of soldiers attacked. Geronimo fled on foot. Twenty Apaches died. The Mexicans enslaved thirty-five. Among the captives was Geronimo's wife Chee-Hash-Kish. He never saw her again. Geronimo stated, "After the treachery and massacre of Casas Grandes, we did not reassemble for a long while."[3]

An Apache waits to ambush an Army wagon in the Sierra Madre mountains. Warfare between the Army and the Apaches began in the 1860s.

PLACED ON THE RESERVATION

The years after the Civil War were quiet ones for Geronimo. Cochise discouraged him from raiding. To secure the Southwest, the Army built a chain of forts. From these forts, troops chased the Apaches. They had little success. In 1870, the U.S. government faced facts. The soldiers could never wipe out the Apaches. They let them live in their own lands. The Apaches received tracts at Fort Apache, Camp Verde, Camp Grant, and Ojo Caliente. There they could learn to farm and raise live-stock. Troops would protect the Apaches from hostile whites.

In 1871, General George Crook told the Apaches they must move onto reservations. If they did not move by February 1872, he would attack them. Then General O. O. Howard replaced Crook. A few months later, Geronimo agreed to move. The Chiricahua reservation lay just north of the Mexican border. His band could live in their mountain homeland.

At Apache Pass, agents issued rations once a month. Geronimo's band received twelve steers, plus clothing and supplies. Geronimo did not like being under the eyes of the whites. Soon, he moved his family to join the White Springs Apaches in New Mexico. There, he tired of the peaceful life. Geronimo went to the mountains of Mexico. He lived with Chief Juh and the Nednis. From time to time, he came north to visit friends.

In 1875, the U.S. government had a new plan. All Apaches must live on one reservation. They chose San Carlos in central Arizona. It was an ugly place, located

Indian Agent John Clum said he would never forget the face of Geronimo. He said he had never seen such a look of hate as when he took Geronimo prisoner and put him in chains.

on a gravelly plain. Lines of scrawny cottonwood trees marked the banks of streams. There was little rain. Day after day, dry, hot winds blew dust and gravel. In summer, it reached 110° F in the shade.

On April 22, 1877, Geronimo's band camped outside Warm Springs. Indian Agent John Clum sent them a message. They were to come to Warm Springs for a talk. Clum sat on a porch. Armed police stood on both sides of the Apaches. Clum faced Geronimo and six other

The Army insisted that the Apaches end their raids. They urged the Apaches to learn to farm. Only through the use of irrigation was it possible to grow any crops at San Carlos.

leaders. He said they would have to move to San Carlos. Geronimo replied, "We are not going back to San Carlos with you. Unless you are very careful, you and your Apache police will not go back to San Carlos either. Your bodies will stay here . . . to make food for coyotes."[1]

Clum gave a signal. From hiding, more police ran onto the parade ground. Their rifles were at the ready. Geronimo's thumb eased off the hammer of his rifle. Geronimo stared at him with hatred. Clum took the gun. He told them they were prisoners. Geronimo reached for his knife. A policeman snatched it away. Clum took the Apaches to the blacksmith shop. Soon, irons linked by chains shackled their ankles.

The Apaches began the long walk to San Carlos. The trip took three weeks. The shackled men rode in a wagon. At San Carlos, Clum kept the leaders in the guard house. He wanted them tried and hanged. The others were free to live anywhere on the reservation. After a few months, a new agent set the leaders free.

Life was bad at San Carlos. The Apaches had poor housing, no food, and not enough clothing. Many died from smallpox and malaria. In September, over 300 fled. On April 4, 1878, Geronimo followed. It was his first of many breakouts.

LIVING ON THE RUN

Geronimo led his band toward the Mexican-U.S. border. It lay over 150 miles to the south. The Apaches moved quickly. They knew the soldiers would follow. The band crossed paths with a wagon train. They killed its drivers. Then they stuffed themselves with captured food. Using fresh horses, they raced on.

Just north of the border, sixty soldiers of the Fourth Cavalry blocked their route. The women and children escaped through a pass in the hills. Geronimo and his warriors retreated up a gully. Near the top, they placed themselves behind rocks. The warriors fired slowly, saving their bullets. Two hours later, the Apaches slipped away. Each went his own way. When the soldiers charged, they found the hilltop empty. Sixty trails led in sixty directions. That night, the Apaches covered almost thirty miles. The band reunited in Mexico.

The Apaches straggled in a column two miles long. With no warning, 250 Mexican troops attacked them. Geronimo had only 32 warriors. Still, the warriors held them off. That night, the Apaches set the grass on fire. They escaped in the smoke.

At last they reached the Sierra Madres. Troops could not safely follow them into the mountains. Some peaks reached to 12,000 feet. Underbrush choked the deep ravines. From the valleys, secret paths led to nearby villages. There the Apaches traded. They sold stolen horses and cattle, and bought supplies and guns.

The Apaches felt free. They could live as they wished. They could go where they wanted. Gone was the ugliness of San Carlos. Gone were white people's rules. Still,

The horse gave the Apaches the mobility they needed to survive in the harsh, arid Southwest. The Apaches often raided Army posts to obtain the animals they needed as replacement and breeding stock.

life was hard for Geronimo's band. Each day they feared that troops would find them. They posted guards every night. Food was scarce. During the winter months, they nearly starved.

With sadness, Geronimo decided to return to San Carlos. There, at least, no one would try to kill his people in the night. In January 1880, he went to the outpost of Camp Rucker. Geronimo approached the officer in command. He promised to lead his band back to San Carlos.

He did not stay at San Carlos long. In August 1881, Geronimo heard a rumor. It said the soldiers would hang him. The next month, he and seventy-four followers fled again. Geronimo's escape made headlines. Cochise was dead. Soldiers had murdered Mangas Coloradas. Now, they said, a new fierce chief led the Apaches. Geronimo led all the Apache bands that were in Mexico.

For the next two years, Geronimo raided north across the border. Each time he grew bolder. A war party came within ten miles of Tombstone, Arizona. A few days later, the war party approached Lordsburg.

In the fall of 1882, General Crook received his orders. He was to pursue Geronimo, even into Mexico. Crook did away with slow-moving wagons. Hardy pack mules carried his supplies. Apache scouts agreed to lead Crook's force to Geronimo's hiding place.

The troops approached the Sierra Madres. They passed the ruins of small towns destroyed by the Apaches. On May 15, 1883, Crook's men reached

Geronimo's secret camp. The Apaches were amazed that Crook had found them. The warriors were out on raids. First the women and children gave up. A few days later, Geronimo agreed to talk with Crook. They sat on the ground and talked. After two hours, Geronimo agreed to surrender. Over the next few days, more Apaches gave up. On May 24, 1883, Geronimo and over 230 Apaches started north to San Carlos.

When Geronimo was taken prisoner, his wife and child went with him to San Carlos. Geronimo had several wives and many children.

GERONIMO'S FINAL BREAKOUTS

Life at San Carlos improved. Geronimo's band lived at Turkey Creek near Fort Apache. Here they found clear water and pine forests. Game was plentiful. The U.S. government wanted the Apaches to become farmers. The agents gave them plows, seeds, and tools. The plan failed. The warriors thought farming was below them. They left such work to women.

The Apaches brewed *tiswin*, a beer made from corn. When they drank, the Apaches got into fights. The Army passed rules against making *tiswin*, as well as on many other things. These limits on their freedoms angered the Apaches. They hated reservation life. They decided to become free.

On May 17, 1885, Geronimo again led his band south. Headlines read: "The Apaches Are Out!" A reporter asked Lieutenant Charles Gatewood, "How many

Apaches are in the field?" "Just forty-two [men] and about ninety [women] and children," Gatewood answered.[1]

En route to the border, the Apaches killed seventeen settlers. Some died during raids. The Apaches killed others to keep them from reporting their presence. Within months, 2,000 soldiers and scouts searched for the Apaches. Geronimo raided throughout the Southwest and northern Mexico. In six weeks (November through December 1885), his band traveled 1,200 miles. During that time, they killed thirty-eight more people. They also stole 250 horses and mules. For months, the Apaches eluded the troops. In January 1886, Army scouts found Geronimo's hideout in Mexico. They captured all his horses and supplies. The band scattered. They moved north, close to the border. Geronimo sent word to Crook. He wanted a meeting.

On March 25, 1886, Geronimo's band met with Crook. Crook reminded them of Geronimo's promise that peace would last. Crook told Geronimo what would happen if he gave up. He would serve two years in prison in the East. Then he could go back to his people. On March 27, Geronimo surrendered. A day later, he heard a rumor that the soldiers would hang him at the border. He fled into the mountains. Only thirty-eight Apaches went with him.

Geronimo's escape angered President Grover Cleveland. He wanted Geronimo hanged. Crook resigned and

General Nelson Miles replaced him. Miles dismissed the Apache scouts. He massed 5,000 troops, a fourth of the entire army. The soldiers fanned out across the Southwest and northern Mexico. They could not find Geronimo. Miles rehired the Apache scouts. This time, the soldiers said, we will find and defeat him.

In late August, the Army had success. Scouts saw a woman from Geronimo's band. She was loading three ponies with supplies. They tracked her to a nearby canyon.

The scouts came to Geronimo under a white flag. They told him, "The troops are coming after you from all directions. They aim to kill everyone of you if it takes fifty years. Everything is against you. If you awake at night and a rock rolls down the mountain or a stick

The Army made good use of Apache Scouts. They knew how to track Geronimo's band across the deserts and into the mountains. It was they who located Geronimo's last hiding place.

Geronimo, shown here with Natchez, was almost 60 when he made his final surrender in 1886. General Miles had promised he could settle in Arizona. Instead, he was sent to prison in Florida.

breaks, you will be running. You even eat your meals running. You have no friends whatever in the world."[2] Geronimo agreed. He asked to talk with Miles.

The two men met on September 3, 1886. Miles told Geronimo that the Army had sent his band to Florida. If he gave up, he could join them within five days. The next day, Geronimo gave himself up. "This is the fourth time I have surrendered," he said. "And I think it is the last," Miles replied.[3] He and Miles placed a large stone on a blanket. The peace, they agreed, would last until the stone crumbled.

GERONIMO'S LATER YEARS

A train carried the Apaches to Fort Marion, Florida. The Apaches lived for a while on the beach. They waited while a well was drilled in the fort. A healthy diet and cleanliness were hard to come by. Rations were cut twice in 1886. Two bath tubs served 469 people. The Apaches died from disease and fevers. Among them was Geronimo's four-year-old daughter. Many Apaches died from tuberculosis.

These once-active people now lived a life of idleness. The women prepared meals and made clothing. The men had no chance to work. Their only task was to keep the place clean. The Army forced some of the youths to attend Carlisle Indian School.

Crook and others protested the treatment of the Apaches. In April 1887, President Cleveland acted. He sent the Apaches to Mount Vernon Barracks, Alabama.

There, Geronimo rejoined his family. He said, "We were not healthy in this place. The climate disagreed with us."[1] A doctor said Apache lungs could not withstand the dampness. Many caught tuberculosis. Others suffered from malaria. By 1889, one fourth of the Apaches had died. Still the Army kept the Apaches at Mount Vernon for six years.

The Army took the Apaches by train from Arizona to Florida. At Fort Marion, many Apaches sickened and died. A year later, the government sent the survivors to Alabama.

Unable to read or write, Geronimo had to dictate his life story. Daklugie interpreted as biographer S.M. Barrett wrote down the remembrances of the great Apache chief.

In 1893, the Army moved the Apaches to Fort Sill. Here, in the Indian Territory (now Oklahoma), they grew corn, melons, and squash. Grasslands fed their cattle. Yet it was not their native homeland. The Apaches continued to die of despair and disease.

Geronimo was still well known. People wanted to see the famous old warrior. Some paid money to do so. On a trip to Omaha, crowds greeted him at each trainstop. They saw an old Apache dressed in white man's clothes. They found it hard to think of him as a feared warrior.

He sold them the buttons off his jacket for twenty-five cents each. Then he sewed on new buttons to sell at the next stop.

In 1904, Geronimo attended the World's Fair in St. Louis. He sold autographed photos and handmade bows. He met with General Miles. Geronimo said that the acorns, piñon nuts, wild turkeys, and giant cactus all missed him in Arizona. Miles said that might be true. But the people there could sleep at night knowing he was elsewhere.

In 1905, Geronimo rode in the inaugural parade of Theodore Roosevelt. He told the President, "Great Father. White men are in the country that was my

Geronimo never was allowed to return to this beloved home range. He hoped to be buried in the mountains of the Southwest. His final resting place is this grave in the Apache Cemetery at Fort Sill.

home. I pray you to tell them to go away. Let my people go there and be happy."[2] Roosevelt said the Apaches would remain at Fort Sill.

In 1906, Geronimo told the story of his long life. A young teacher wrote it down. Geronimo wanted the public to know his side of events. Then, he hoped, they would support his wish to go home.

Geronimo lived in despair and depression. In February 1909, he rode alone to a nearby town. The weather was cold, the ground icy. Against the rules, he bought a bottle of whiskey. Geronimo drank heavily. He fell from his horse into a watery ditch. By morning, he was very ill. He died three days later. He was buried at Fort Sill.

In 1912, Congress allowed some of the Apaches to go back to the Southwest. In April of that year, a small group of 187 Apaches returned at last to their beloved New Mexico hills. Some of Geronimo's family still live near Fort Sill. The Apaches have not forgotten their famous leader.

NOTES BY CHAPTER

Chapter 1

1. Alexander B. Adams, *Geronimo* (New York: G.P. Putnam's Sons, 1971), pp. 84–85.

Chapter 2

1. S. M. Barrett, *Geronimo, His Own Story* (New York: E.P. Dutton, 1970), p. 82.

Chapter 3

1. Sam Haozous interview, *Geronimo, The Man, His Time, His Place* (Norman: University of Oklahoma, 1976), p. 38.

2. Barrett, pp. 90–91.

3. Ibid.

Chapter 5

1. Angie Debo, *Geronimo, The Man, His Time, His Place* (Norman: University of Oklahoma Press, 1976), p. 66.

2. David Jeffrey, *Geronimo* (Milwaukee: Raintree Publishers, 1990), p. 22.

3. Barrett, p. 115.

Chapter 6

1. Debo, p. 105.

Chapter 8

1. Odie Faulk, *The Geronimo Campaign* (New York: Oxford University Press, 1969), p. 62.

2. Morris Opler, "A Chiricahua Apache's Account of the Geronimo Campaign of 1886," *New Mexico Historical Review*, Vol. XIII, No. 4 (October 1938), pp. 375–377.

3. Nelson Miles, *Personal Recollections* (New York: Werner, 1897), pp. 526–527.

Chapter 9

1. Zachary Kent, *The Story of Geronimo* (Chicago: Children's Press, 1989), p. 28.

2. Russell Shorto, *Geronimo and the Struggle for Apache Freedom* (Englewood Cliffs, NJ: Silver Burdett, 1989), p. 124.

GLOSSARY

band—A subdivision of a tribe, often only a few dozen in number.

breastworks—Low walls, often shoulder high, used in defense or ambush.

cavalry—Troops mounted on horses.

Chihuahua—A northern Mexican state.

Chiracahua—A band of Apaches led by Cochise and Geronimo.

Civil War—The 1861–1865 struggle between the northern (Union) and southern (Confederate) states.

cougar—A large tawny brown cat also known as a mountain lion.

malaria—A mosquito-carried disease causing high fever and death.

rations—Food and supplies issued on a regular basis.

reservation—An area set aside to serve as a tribal homeland.

shrapnel—Fragments of an exploding artillery shell.

Sierra Madres—A mountain range of northern Mexico parallel to the Pacific Coast.

Sonora—A northwestern Mexican state.

Southwest—The area that includes west Texas, Arizona, and New Mexico.

tipi—A conical structure made up of hides over a pole frame.

tuberculosis—An often fatal disease of the lungs.

warrior—An adult male in Native American cultures responsible for hunting and warfare.

MORE GOOD READING ABOUT
═══════════GERONIMO═══════════

Adams, Alexander. *Geronimo*. New York: G.P. Putnam's Sons, 1971.

Barrett, S. M. *Geronimo, His Own Story*. New York: E.P. Dutton, 1970.

Capps, Benjamin. *The Great Chiefs*. New York: Time-Life Books, 1975.

Debo, Angie. *Geronimo, The Man, His Time, His Place*. Norman, Okla.: University of Oklahoma, 1976.

Faulk, Odie. *The Geronimo Campaign*. New York: Oxford University Press, 1969.

Jeffrey, David. *Geronimo*. Milwaukee: Raintree Publishers, 1990.

Kent, Zachary. *The Story of Geronimo*. Chicago: Children's Press, 1989.

Kjelgaard, Jim. *The Story of Geronimo*. New York: Grosset & Dunlap, 1958.

Mails, Thomas. *The People Called Apache*. Englewood Cliffs, N.J.: Prentice-Hall, 1974.

Shorto, Russell. *Geronimo and the Struggle for Apache Freedom*. Englewood Cliffs, N.J.: Silver Burdett, 1989.

Stahl, Ben. *Geronimo, The Fighting Apache*. New York: William Morrow, 1975.

Thrapp, Dan. *Al Seiber, Chief of Scouts*. Norman, Okla.: University of Oklahoma Press, 1964.

Thrapp, Dan. *The Conquest of Apacheria*. Norman, Okla.: University of Oklahoma Press, 1967

INDEX